CONTENTS

Words in **bold** are in the glossary.

TRAVEL AROUND THE WORLD

Around the world, people need to get from place to place. They take short trips to work. They visit markets. Some take long trips. They visit family. All use many types of **transport**.

In cities, people may travel by buses or trains. Some drive cars. People in the **countryside** may ride horses. They may drive cars too.

Customs Around the World

TRANSPORT
Around the World

by Lindsay Shaffer

raintree
a Capstone company — publishers for children

Raintree is an imprint of Capstone Global Library Limited, a company incorporated in England and Wales having its registered office at 264 Banbury Road, Oxford, OX2 7DY – Registered company number: 6695582

www.raintree.co.uk
myorders@raintree.co.uk

Edited by Abby Huff
Designed by Julie Peters
Original illustrations © Capstone Global Library Limited 2022
Picture research by Jo Miller
Production by Spencer Rosio
Originated by Capstone Global Library Ltd
Printed and bound in India

978 1 3982 0270 2 (hardback)
978 1 3982 0269 6 (paperback)

British Library Cataloguing in Publication Data
A full catalogue record for this book is available from the British Library.

Acknowledgements
We would like to thank the following for permission to reproduce photographs: Alamy: imageBROKER, 21, Mike Goldwater, 19; Getty Images: NurPhoto/Contributor, 13; iStockphoto: wanderluster, 17; Shutterstock: Aleksandar Todorovic, 24-25, barteverett, 1, BrandonKleinVideo, 6, caminel, 26, G Allen Penton, 23, Hiromi Ito Ame, 18, I. Noyan Yilmaz, 20, Joseph Sohm, 10-11, lkoimages, 15, meunierd, 9, MVolodymyr, 28, phantomm, 12, QOcreative, 7, RickDeacon, 27, S-F, 8, Suparin, 5, Witthaya lOvE, Cover. Design elements: Capstone; Shutterstock: Stawek (map), VLADGRIN

Every effort has been made to contact copyright holders of material reproduced in this book. Any omissions will be rectified in subsequent printings if notice is given to the publisher.

All the internet addresses (URLs) given in this book were valid at the time of going to press. However, due to the dynamic nature of the internet, some addresses may have changed, or sites may have changed or ceased to exist since publication. While the author and publisher regret any inconvenience this may cause readers, no responsibility for any such changes can be accepted by either the author or the publisher.

People in Thailand
waiting for a bus

Water surrounds some towns.

People there use boats to travel.

How do you get from place to place?

IN THE CITY

Cities are busy places. Many people live close together. They need a lot of ways to get around. Trains can carry hundreds of people. Most run on a steel track. Some run underground.

The **subway** in New York City in the United States is a famous underground train system. Millions of people use it each day. Have you been on a train?

A subway train arrives at Penn Station in New York.

A maglev train in Shanghai, China

Shanghai, China, has the fastest train in the world. It's called a maglev train. The train uses magnets to lift into the air. Other magnets push and pull the train. It travels at up to 430 kilometres (267 miles) per hour! The ride is smooth and quiet.

Buses travel through cities and countrysides. Many people travel by bus every day. Double-decker buses move through the streets of London. People take them to work or school. They use them to go shopping. **Tourists** go on buses to see the city.

Double-decker buses in London

A micro

Buses weave through the streets of Lima, Peru. The bus system is called *El Metropolitano*. The buses run along set **routes**. But they do not go all over the city. Many people take smaller buses. These are called micros. Some take vans called combis.

Does your family travel by car? In Los Angeles, California, USA, many people drive cars. This causes a lot of **traffic**. People can spend hours stuck on the road!

People also use car shares and taxis.
Car shares can be free or cost money.
The cars are owned by the drivers. Taxi
drivers use cars owned by a company.
Journeys by taxi always cost money.
Using car shares and taxis means
fewer cars on the roads.

City streets are often jammed with cars and buses. Smaller types of transport can move faster through traffic. In Thailand, tuk tuks are popular. Tuk tuks only have three wheels. They are open on each side. People take them through crowded streets.

A tuk tuk

A motorbike on a busy road in Lagos

Many people around the world use motorbikes. These speedy bikes cost much less than cars. They are smaller than motorcycles. People take them through the busy streets of Lagos, Nigeria. People there even ride motorbike taxis!

Have you ever ridden your bike to school? People in Copenhagen, Denmark, do.

Copenhagen even has bicycle highways! People can rent bikes or electric scooters. This makes it easy to avoid traffic jams. Scooters and bikes can zip past **stationary** cars.

ANIMAL TRANSPORT

Many people live far from cities. Some live on farms or ranches. Others live on mountains or in deserts. Some places have few roads. In places like these, people often ride animals.

In the United States, some people work on cattle ranches. Cattle travel over many kilometres of land. Ranchers ride horses to guide and lead cattle. Horses can go places cars cannot. They can walk in water. They can climb rocky ground. Have you ever been on a horse?

In the mountains of Tibet, people use yaks. Yaks can carry heavy packs. Their strong backs can hold hundreds of kilograms! They can walk long distances too. They help people carry supplies to mountain villages.

People in Somalia ride camels. These animals travel easily across the desert. They also help people move goods. Camels can carry over 90 kilograms (200 pounds)!

IN THE SNOW

In Antarctica, snow and ice cover the ground all year. The ice can be very thick. Sometimes it's over a kilometre deep! People use snowmobiles to get around. Snowmobiles can seat one or two people. Some can travel at speeds of more than 241 kph (150 mph)!

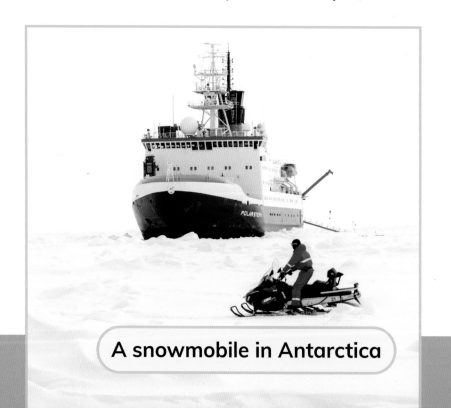

A snowmobile in Antarctica

A dog sledge team in Greenland

Winter in Greenland brings thick layers of ice and snow. Dog sledges help people get across the frozen land. **Mushers** attach their dogs to sledges using ropes. Then, they stand on the back of the sledges. They shout a **command**. The dogs take off, pulling the sledges behind them!

IN THE AIR

Have you flown in an aeroplane? Some planes carry hundreds of people! Others seat only a handful of people.

In Alaska, many people own planes. There are few roads for cars and buses. People fly planes to travel to other towns. The planes are small. Many can land on water!

A plane parked on water in Alaska

La Paz, Bolivia, rests in the mountains. Many people there ride cable cars. Cable cars cost less than buses. They carry people high above the ground to a city called El Alto. It takes 10 minutes to get there.

Cable cars travelling over La Paz

The cable cars hang from long steel cables. The cables move the cars forward. They are strung between tall poles. At each end, the cars arrive at stations. There, people get on and off.

ON THE WATER

Some places in the world are surrounded by water. Venice, Italy, is a city built on islands. Instead of roads, waterways called **canals** weave through the city. Long, thin boats help people get around. The boats are called gondolas.

Gondolas on a canal in Venice

A ferry in Sydney

A big river runs through the middle of Sydney, Australia. Many people travel over it. They take **ferries**. These big boats carry passengers on short trips. Some of them carry cars too. Would you like to travel by boat?

People use many types of transport. This depends on where they live. Some people live in places that are hard to get to. They might use planes. Others ride animals. People in big cities take trains. What are your favourite ways to travel?

MAP

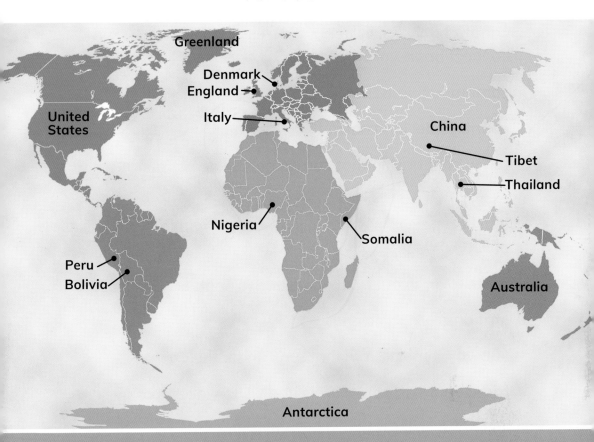

Greenland

Denmark
England

United
States

Italy

China

Tibet

Thailand

Nigeria

Somalia

Peru
Bolivia

Australia

Antarctica

Around the world, there are many ways to travel. See which places were talked about in this book!

GLOSSARY

canal channel of water dug across land; canals connect bodies of water

command word that tells what to do

countryside land not in towns or cities

ferry boat or ship that carries people across a stretch of water

musher person who travels over snow with a sledge pulled by dogs

route plan to get from one place to another

stationary not moving

subway type of train that runs under the ground

tourist person who travels and visits places for fun

traffic vehicles that are moving on a road

transport way to move from one place to another

FIND OUT MORE

BOOKS

Getting Around Through the Years: How Transport Has Changed in Living Memory (History in Living Memory), Clare Lewis (Raintree, 2016)

Our World in Pictures: Cars, Trains, Ships and Planes: A Visual Encyclopedia to Every Vehicle, DK (DK Children, 2015)

Trains (Transport), Mari Schuh (Raintree, 2017)

WEBSITE

www.dkfindout.com/uk/transport
Find out more about different types of transport.

INDEX